Baron de Wolffers

## Turkey's Fall the Decline of England

A Suggestion and a Warning to Turkish Bondholders and Russian

Moneylenders

Baron de Wolffers

**Turkey's Fall the Decline of England**
*A Suggestion and a Warning to Turkish Bondholders and Russian Moneylenders*

ISBN/EAN: 9783744696760

Printed in Europe, USA, Canada, Australia, Japan

Cover: Foto ©ninafisch / pixelio.de

More available books at **www.hansebooks.com**

# Turkey's Fall the Decline of England.

## A SUGGESTION AND A WARNING TO TURKISH BONDHOLDERS AND RUSSIAN MONEY-LENDERS.

BY

FR. BARON DE WOLFFERS, Phil. and LL.D.,

*Knight of the Order of Merit of Bavaria, Officer of the Order of the Saviour, Commander of the Nichan Iftihar.*

London:

JOHN KEMPSTER & CO.,

9 and 10, ST. BRIDE'S AVENUE, FLEET STREET, E.C.

1875.

Hazell, Watson, & Viney, Printers, London and Aylesbury.

# PREFACE TO SECOND EDITION.

THE day after the first edition of our pamphlet left the press the *Daily Telegraph* published a letter from Henry Stanley, dated from Mtesa's Capital, Uganda, April 15th, 1875.

To our great satisfaction the worthy successor of Livingstone commends warmly the mode of colonization proposed by ourselves for Turkey, and almost in the same words.

We extract the following passages from the gallant travellers's letters :—

" Mtesa has caused the ten commandments of Moses to be written on a board for his daily perusal—for Mtesa can read Arabic—as well as the Lord's Prayer and the golden commandment of Our Saviour," ' Thou shalt love thy neighbour as thyself.' This is great progress for the few days that I have remained with him, and, though I am no missionary, I shall begin to think that I might become one if such success is feasible. But, oh that some pious, practical missionary would come here ! What a field and a harvest ripe for the sickle of Civilisation ! Mtesa would give him anything he desired—houses, lands, cattle, ivory, &c., he might call a province his own in one day. It is not the mere preacher, however, that is wanted here. The Bishops of Great Britain collected, with all the classic youth of Oxford and Cambridge, would effect nothing by mere talk with the people of Uganda. It is the practical Christian tutor, who can teach people how to become Christians, cure their diseases, construct dwellings, understand and exemplify agriculture, and turn his hand to anything, like a sailor—this is the man who is wanted. Such an one if he can be found would become the saviour of Africa. He must be tied to no Church or Sect, but profess God and His Son and the moral law, and live a blameless Christian, inspired by liberal principles, charity to all men, and devout faith in Heaven. He must belong to no nation in particular, but the entire white race. Such a man or men Mtesa, King of Uganda, Usoga, Umgoro, and Karagwe—a kingdom 360 geographical miles in length by 50 in breadth—invites to repair to him. He has begged me to tell the white men that if they will only come to him he will give them all they want. For the mission's use it should bring with it a supply of hammers, saws, augers, chisels, axes, hatchets, adzes, carpenters' and blacksmiths' tools, since the Waganda are apt pupils ; iron drills and powder for blasting purposes, trowels, a couple of good-sized anvils, a forge and bellows, an assortment of nails and tacks, a plough, spades, shovels, pickaxes, and a couple of light buggies as specimens, with such other small things as their own common sense would suggest to the men whom I invite. Most desirable would be an assortment of garden seed and grain ; also white-lead, linseed oil, brushes, a few volumes of illustrated journals, gaudy prints, a magic lantern, rockets, and a photographic apparatus. The total cost of the whole equipment need not exceed five thousand pounds sterling.

HENRY M. STANLEY."

We have been most happy to see Stanley's plan meet in England with the sympathy and encouragement it fully de-serves, but far from lessening the interest which England may feel in our plan of colonising a part of Turkey; it con-secrates, if I may say so, its practicability, and we have shown that it was a political necessity. Mr. Stanley states that the colonisation of King Mtesa's vast dominions could be realised at an expense of five thousand pounds sterling, and bring great profit to our industry and commerce. Wonders would be done in Turkey by following our plan, with, say £15000 or £20,000 not spent but simply *advanced* on the best security, and it would seem from a correspondent of the *Echo*, in a letter dated Constantinople, November 4th, that the *nucleus* of the colony could be found already in Turkey itself under the following circumstances :—

The correspondent is informed that the greatest misery prevails at Sophia amongst the workmen, engineers, and foremen, who are engaged by the government for the Sophia Railroad, the works of which have been discontinued. Foreigners have no means of returning, and what they will do throughout this harsh winter, when they are at times in trouble for a morsel of bread I do not like to think of.

Probable as it is that these destitute men are Englishmen, it would be an act of national justice and charity, in the right moment and the right place, to enlist them for a colony des-tined to reflect credit on its founders, and become a lasting benefit for England. As to what we said about ultramontane propaganda in non-christian parts, we find it illustrated in the following extract from a Paris correspondent of the *Daily Telegraph* of November 17th, 1875.

The *Conseil Général* of Algiers is alarmed at the zeal of missionaries in Kabylia. The Prefect treats these fears as absurd, and the Archbishop denounces them as impious. A correspondent of the *Journal des Débats* tells us some of the facts which create uneasiness. It seems that ten years since Marshal Macmahon, then Governor General, had to complain of a dangerous zeal in proselitysing. The matter was referred home. On one hand, devout ladies in Paris preferred *neuvaines* for the Marshal's enlightenment, on the other the government, instructed the Archbishop to moderate his activity.

When the famine happened, many Arab parents trusted their children to the priests. A great number of orphans also were received by them. These children the Archbishop refused to give up when their friends claimed them. Upon appeal to the courts he was defeated, but the fruits of victory remained with the Church, for the Archbishop exacted repayment of all expenses before surrendering the children, and few Arabs could or would discharge the debt. Very many orphans were sent to Marseilles, and others were established in the large mission farms. In Kabylia leave was given to set up *maisons de charité*—relieving houses as they may be called. But to each of these a school has been added. Religious opinion is declared sacred therein, but the scholars learn hymns addressed to the virgin, and they are taught the Catholic faith upon demand. The discontent aroused amongst a Moslem population by these doings has stirred the *Conseil Général* to vote 20,000 francs for a secular school in Kabylia. It is said that an emigration has begun towards Tunis and Morocco; some notable families, who had shown good will to France, have gone. At the same time it is alleged that the priests fail entirely in their efforts, whilst causing such a serious agitation.

That the Turkish Government is good willed, results from the following communication which reached Berlin, on December 5th :—

" The Circular Note sent by Reshid Pasha to Turkish diplomatic agents, states that the Ottoman Government is resolved to introduce and carry out all internal reforms, and will gladly accept advice from the Great Powers in respect to such reforms.

We insisted on seeing as it were fresh blood infused in the veins of Turkish administration by the accession of able and honest Englishmen to high and influential posts in Turkey, to do away with the leper which gnaws at the heart of the state, and which is most strikingly and veraciously characterised by the Constantinople correspondent of the *Daily Telegraph*, quoted by that contemporary in its number of December 1st of this year.

" As the military power of the Turks has waned, and as a bureaucracy has grown up with all the faults and none of the energy and vigour of that institution in civilised countries, the condition of the Christians in Turkey has deteriorated from year to year. They have not even gained by the successes of some among their own number. The emancipation of the Greeks has merely given freedom to a race of plunderers by profession, who are avenging themselves for long years of servitude by fleecing alike their ancient masters and their former comrades in slavery. Nor have the Christian peasants profited by the rise of many Armenians to power ; for these wolves in sheep's clothing are to the full as grasping, as luxurious, and as unscrupulous as the most overbearing and sensual of the Turks, and they have introduced into the Empire, and into the palaces of its rulers, an extravagance and a reckless profusion of which the older Turks knew nothing. and out of which the Armenians have known well how to make enormous profits at the expense of the suffering thousands who have long groaned under a taxation which is now intolerable.

After all that has been written on the acquisition by England of the shares of the Khedive in the Canal of Suez, there remains the simple fact, that England, by its purchase, has established her influence over Egypt on a largerbasis than before.

And why should not private enterprise do for England in Turkey what the English Government realized in Egypt?

The ground is quite prepared as it results from a correspondence in the *Daily Telegraph,* under the 24th of Nov.:—

"The Sultan has on more than one occasion tried to do good. When he returned from England, he was bitten with a desire to improve the agriculture of his country. At the same time his visit to the Zoological Gardens had aroused in him the desire, which is never long dormant in an Eastern Prince, for a collection of wild animals. He determined to establish on the hill which overlooks Ortakein an institution which should combine the solid usefulness of the model farms at Windsor with the *bizarre* delights of the Regent's Park. In obedience to his will there soon arose, at a convenient distance from his favourite residence, a range of farm buildings at sight of which Mr. Mechi would have hid his diminished head and thrown down his bucolic pen for ever. The choicest breeds of cattle and sheep, the finest strains of poultry, the most efficient forms of agricultural implements, and the latest and best devices for making two blades of grass where but one had grown before, there found representatives. There also were gathered all the zoological monstrosities of the East, treasures of which a Jamrach might be jealous, beasts of which a Buckland might boast.

"For a time the hobby prospered, and, if the model farm could have been steadily maintained with something less of luxury, and with a closer application to the real wants of the country, it might in the long course of years have done much good; but after a while the Sultan grew weary, a murrain robbed the establishment of its choicest cattle, whose carcases infected the hillsides for months, and the undertaking came to an end. The buildings are still kept up, as no buildings which belong to the Sultan are suffered to fall out of repair; but the wild beasts have for the most part been removed to Beicos, and little remains of the original enterprise save a few patches of cultivated land which have not yet lost the fertility they acquired when the good work was young and prosperous."

How easily could the representatives of the English-Turkish bondholders get possession of these neglected establishments, and from that splendid beginning go on with their work of civilisation and progress.

But Turkey is a land of promise for the plan we propose. Let us hear what a correspondent of the *Standard* relates: (See that paper of December 10th).

"Turkey ought to be the favoured seat of the goddess of agriculture. Its long ranges of hills and valleys, which succeed each other without interruption, and its climate, which is so varied as to be favourable alike to the products of the temperate and to those of the torrid zone, give it such advantages as hardly any other empire possesses. But despite the charms of its climate and the fertility of its soil, agriculture languishes under the want of capital, the ignorance of the cultivators, and the absence of roads. Even where roads exist, as for instance along the entire line of railway from Constantinople to Adrianople, the fertility of the soil and the facility of transport are entirely neutralized by the want of skill and capital on the side of the cultivators, and by the exactions of the agents of the Government. Some branches of agriculture which might be profitably cultivated have been altogether neglected. Oats are not grown, barley being used instead of oats as food for horses and cattle. Roots are almost unknown, so that fat cattle are equally unknown, whilst many perish annually through the insufficiency or the bad quality of their pasture. Rice, which is largely consumed throughout the empire, and which would grow well in many districts, is for the most part imported from Egypt and Italy. Wheat is grown in considerable, though not in sufficient quantities, but much is wasted in the threshing, or perhaps I should say in the treading, for the agricultural machinery of Turkey does not yet include that very old-fashioned implement, a flail. When the wheat is threshed, or trodden out, the means of grinding it are of the most primitive kind, and the greater part of the flour which we consume in Constantinople has travelled in the shape of grain from Odessa to England, and returned hither after receiving the necessary preparation."

The entire agricultural system of the country is at fault. In former days a Turkish landed proprietor divided his land into three portions, and allowed each to lie fallow in turn. By this means he obtained fair crops without the aid of manure. Now, the unhappy rayah labours at his small plot from year to year, and has no idea of enriching it by aid of manure, thought an abundance of that kind of matter, which is useless only when it is in the wrong place, lies in heaps in his native village, and infects the hamlet instead of enriching the fields. When his overworked land will no longer yield a crop he goes forth to the neighbouring forest, where, unhappily. he has a right of clearance, and burns down hundreds of valuable trees. Having, by much labour, obtained an additional plot of arable land, he begins once more to crop it, until it is exhausted, after which he sets to work again to destroy another portion of the forest and to misuse the soil which he wrests from it. It is believed by competent judges that the wholesale destruction of the Turkish forests during the last thirty years has sensibly affected the climate of the country, and threatens to induce a serious deficiency of moisture. Certain it is that a remarkable increase has taken place in the price of firewood in Constantinople, and that the friends of Turkey are beginning to console themselves for this augmentation in the price of a necessary of life with the reflection that when there is no more wood or charcoal for the stoves and the mangals, the Turks will be forced to work their coal mines, and thus pave the way for the introduction of a hundred industries which depend for their existence on coal. Waiting this desirable consummation the forests perish, the industries are not born, and agriculture lies bound hand and foot."

And it is not only agriculture that offers a large field to English enterprise, there are many excellent openings in and about Constantinople itself, out of which the bondholders could reap immense profits. We refer again to a correspondence in the *Daily Telegraph* of November 24th.

" There is a fine field for moderate honest tradesmen, and an hotelkeeper with a conscience and an appreciation for the wants of his guests would soon make a fortune. We want gas, we want water, we want roads and pavements, we want better means of transport from place to place ; and we could pay a fair price for these advantages if any enterprising person would confer them on us. But the past history of enterprise in this city is not encouraging. One only has succeeded, and it is perhaps a curious circumstance that the Sultana Valide is largely interested in it  The steamboats which ply on the Bosphorus throughout the day, and which are commodious and admirably well conducted return a good interest to the shareholders, and her Highness is the largest holder of shares. The tramways, on the other hand, though the carriages are always full, are unremunerative, the undertaking having been swamped at the outset by the overfinancing of its capital. Again, the concession for the erection of wharves and warehouses, which are sorely needed, has been nullified by the interposition of all sorts of petty obstacles ; whilst the scheme for the water supply hangs fire because it is supposed that the water will be too pure to suit the popular taste. Lastly, the enormous traffic across the Golden Horn, which yields an almost fabulous revenue in tolls, is condemned to pass over two rickety and absolutely dangerous bridges, the efforts of the Municipality to provide new bridges having culminated at last in a determination to pull down one which was on the verge of completion. The man who hopes to accomplish any undertaking in this country must bring with him an iron will and a patience compared with which that of Job would seem mere fretful irritability. He should also bring with him, or make up his mind to acquire, a knowledge of the Turkish language. Without this he is lost indeed. Let him not believe that a knowledge of French only will serve his turn. A knowledge of French will enable him to communicate with the Armenians and Greeks and Levantines, but it will not bring him face to face with the real holders of power in this country. If he listens to the Christian members of this community, he will go away with the idea that he need not learn the Turkish language, but that is merely because they want to keep the key of the house in their own pocket. The real holders of power in this country are the Turks, and very few of them speak any language but their own. It is said that the present Grand Vizier has no one in his house who can speak any language but those of the country. Many of the Europeans who come here in search of information with regard to the country are altogether led astray by their ignorance of the language. Mr. Butler Johnstone apparently has gone away with the impression that Midhat Pasha is the cleverest man in Turkey, merely because he and Midhad Pasha speak French, and could understand each other, Here, too, has been Mr. Arthur Kinnard in search of the materials for a speech. Here, too, is my Lord Strathoden, picking up the crumbs which Mr. Kinnard left on the ground ; and here, again, is my Lady Strangford, with a mission for the construction of a railway from Jaffa to Jerusalem, and with a small staff of obedient colonels and captains and professors, who ride over Asia Minor on dromedaries to do her bidding. But all these people are checked and hindered at every turn by their ignorance of the language and by their consequent inability to talk openly with the masters of the country. Therefore let the man who aims at the regeneration of Turkey make up his mind at the very onset of his undertaking to acquire a knowledge of its language."

The Turkish bondholders have held meetings and come to certain resolutions, but alas all their endeavours will prove nothing but—

*Ludere par impar equitare in arundine longa—*

and come what may, in ten or twenty years those who lent their money to Turkey will be obliged to recur to our or to a similar plan. What would be easy now will be very difficult later, and, mayhap impossible, for the Russian Black Eagle may then have made new efforts to seize upon the prey he covets since more than a century.

What we wrote in regard to the Russian moneylenders, receives a striking illustration in a correspondence of the *Daily Telegraph*, stating that the—

"harvest in Russia this year is exceptionally bad, and the grain crop throughout the empire may be taken as a whole at from 10 to 30 per cent. below what is called a fair medium crop. In the neighbourhood of Odessa, and in the province of Kherson, there is not sufficient grain for the support of the peasants during the winter. The same is the case in the province of Tamhof, one of the richest grain-producing regions of Russia, being in the celebrated black-soil country. Last year there was a bad dry autumn, which ruined much of the winter wheat. This was followed by an unusually long winter and an adverse spring, which ruined not only the grain, but the hay. Besides this the cattle disease broke out in many places, so that in Podolia cows are selling for two roubles, and in Kief horses for three ; while in Voronezh the celebrated *bitink* stallions, which ordinarily bring 200 roubles, are now selling for no more than 20. The failure of the harvest has not been able to affect the exports of grain this year, for these are drawn from the last year's crop, but next year we may expect to see shipments sensibly diminish. The suffering in some places has already begun to be great, but, owing to the delay in the receipt of Government statistics, the exact state of the case cannot yet be known. The provencial and district diets have done something to relieve the distress, but the Government will be obliged to come to the rescue by forbearing to collect arrears of taxes, and in many cases remitting the taxes entirely for a year or two. The bad harvests which afflict the South of Russia are now almost periodical at intervals of three or four years, and are traced by many to the gradual exhaustion of the soil, the wanton destruction of forests, and the lack of moisture. It is therefore urged upon the Government to take measures for tree-planting on a large scale, and for constructing irrigating canals—a work which can be easily done. In fact, one or two irrigation companies have alread sought charters, but the usual departmental delays have hitherto prevented their receiving them."

Without her agriculture Russia's banner would fall to the ground ; we have shown how that backbone of Russia's force is eaten up by gangrene, and that Russia is doomed to become more and more impoverished on its certain way to bankruptcy. Yet at Petersburg they dream of conquests, of extending Russian sway far and wide, for the curse of mankind, for there is nothing more perverse than Russian rule, whether of German or Muscovite origin, and England must blush every inch of ground lost to her interest, and consequently lost to civilization, by becoming a prey to Russian barbarism.

Russia, after having been the instigator, is now the key-stone of a new Triple Alliance, in which Austria plays certainly the part of a dupe, whereas in Berlin they know what they are at; for it is the play of new-born Germany to lull Austria with the prospects of agrandisement in the East, that it may be driven the easier out of its Western German possessions. The Hungarian minister Andrassy is too narrow-minded to see through the plans of the farsighted German Chancellor, who knows very well that Austria has lost on Germany *that* hold she had supreme, when her preponde-rating influence, wielded the German Union (Bund) in Frankfort, before and till 1848. But it was in Frankfort and at that revolutionary period that Prussia came to the consci-ence of her protestant supremacy, and from that moment the doom of the ultramontane Habsburgs as *German* sovereigns was sealed.

Since that time also, Austrian statesmen have lost their compass, and have been tossed about by events and circum-stances which they could neither influence nor control.

It was a great act of wisdom on the part of the present English cabinet to keep aloof from the pact of the three emperors, for in the same time *they* sit before the green cloth more embarrased than the augurs of yore, to look serious at each other, England has really the cards in hand, and all will depend on her for the game to play.

Since we wrote the first edition of this pamphlet, England has made a clever move towards consolidating materially her interest in the Canal of Suez, and in the affairs of Egypt, without in the least compromising herself by any false step in the direction of an annexation.

Although certain English papers, renowned for their fickleness and for their reckless turncoating, have seemed, out of calculated ignorance, to give up Turkey as a hopeless incurable invalid, England and her statesmen know better· The Sultan is not the "sick man" whom Nicholas mentioned disdainfully to Lord Seymour, nor would Englishmen exclaim, with French levity and superficial knowledge of the facts—*les Turcs sont campés en Europe !*

Turkey, numbers in Europe four millions of Mussulman, and six millions of non-Mussulman subjects; but those four million are like ten to every single non-Mussulman ; they are the lords of the land, they are the army, they are the government. The mussulman world looks upon Constantinople as upon its capital, and on the Sultan as its head, and God forbid that the Mussulman Rule should ever be replaced by Russian rottenness on the Danube or the Bosphorus. The integrity of Turkey is as necessary to Europe, as are the first and foremost conditions of Europe's welfare, nay as are the most essential conditions of its progress and civilisation.

To consider The Turks as camped in Europe? indeed! Austria was camped in fact in Italy all the time her cursed rule made the fair Peninsula a hell, she was really camped, for beyond the camp and the barracks in which she was entrenched, she was ·powerless. Not so Turkey. But did the powers who now pretend to interfere in the affairs of Turkey ever interfere when Austria crushed Italy under her brutal heel? Does anybody think to interfere between the Pope and the measures of Prince Bismark. Would England allow anybody to interfere between herself and Ireland?

The Turkish empire justly resents the pretensions of the

powers to establish a guardianship over it, and if they do it under pretence of the Turkish debt, Austria aught to consider that she repudiated her's more than once in the most shameless way; and as to Russia, we have shown, and show in the following pages, what her bondholders may expect.

If any country wanted a guardianship for financial recklessness, for wretched misgovernment, it is Russia. But what would haughty Russia say, if any power tried to interfere for the oppressed Poles, or in favour of her illtreated Catholic and Jewish subjects?

England's statesmen know very well, that Russia does not care the least for the non-Mussulman subjects of the Sultan. She wants a specious pretence for her ambitious views for her projects of conquest and aggrandisement; and therefore England will never let Turkey be humiliated but, keeping on the side of justice she will, by respectful and well-meant advice, bring those measures to bear for the welfare of the Turkish Empire, which no menaces, no threats, no hypocritical cajolery could impose upon the Sublime Porte.

It depends on England to achieve, that the treaty entered into between the three powers, renewed from the whilome Holy Alliance of sinister memory, that that treaty come to no other result than spoiling the parchment on which the ill-omined document is written.

It is because our plan of colonisation could mightily concur to such a desired aim that we brought it before the public far from any thought of imposing a protectorate of whatever kind on the Porte. Coming to the aid of a good friend and trusty ally, by encouragements, by example, by good advice, by going hand in hand with him, would make Turkey bless England, and double her power in the world just where it is her duty to strengthen it most, in erecting an insuperable bulwark against ambitious Russia, and encroaching Austria, warning at the same time Germany, tacitly of the dangers of persisting in a system which estranges the great nation of thinkers from the western world, and drives it to political adventures which must needs end in bitter deceptions.

Let us now clear up, before it arises, a misunderstanding which, at the outset, would compromise our whole project.

When an Englishman, an Irishman, a Scotchman, Frenchman, or a German emigrates to the United States or Australia, to settle there permanently, he becomes *ipso facto* citizen of the state which he chooses for his new country. It is not the case in England, because here foreigners having no right to acquire property, the permanent settlement of a great many of them is out of question, the more so, as almost insuperable obstacles are thrown in the way of naturalisation, and the settlement of Foreigners begins only after a genera-tion, when English born children of Foreigners acquire the rights of English subjects.

No country can tolerate a *state in the state* as it is the pretention of Rome to be wherever she can gain foot. All states who shut their eyes to that fact can no longer boast of their rule prudence.

As to Turkey, it is clear that the members of our colony would become, by the fact of their settlement, as proprietors of Turkish soil, new subjects of the Sultan. And as such, their postion would be an enviable one, for the Christian sub-jects of Turkey have acces to all the positions in the Empire however exalted, and by their skill, industry, honesty and intelligence, they would acquire an influence which would benefit both their adopted country and themselves.

Those who could misunderstand our meaning in that re-spect, had better to remain strangers to the enterprise.

Wisely has England rendered the colonisation of her Empire, by Foreigners, almost an impossibility in the first generation, for that colonisation in relatively so small a community as the English was and is yet, could have become a disguised invasion.

We see it in America, where Irish settlers, on one side, and German settlers on the other, menace the very principles on which the constitution of the United States is based, and that to such an extent, that President Grant, as we see by his *last* message, takes alarm at it.

We therefore maintain, not only that our colonists must become Turkish subjects, but that Turkey ought to oppose our scheme, if it were not thoroughly submitted to this condition *sine qua non*.

We want, in the vital interest of England to stave Turkish independence, Turkish rule instead of undermining it.

The intervention of the Powers, duped by Russia, has done mischief enough already, and it is high time to counteract Russian misrepresentation.

Russian gold exercises on the Press of Germany, and even France, an influence, which we can only call deplorable. England alone never recurs to such means; when the government wants to convey their opinion, it is in an English straightforward way, so that friends and foes alike may know what they are at; and England possesses the immense advantage that, let her cabinet be Whig or Tory, her principles in Foreign affairs are invariable, and her traditions carried out and upheld by the statesmen of both parties, with equal fairness, equal energy, and equal patriotism.

England is now the only Power on which Turkey can rely without distrust, for England always strove manly for the independence of Turkey, and never recognised the conquest of any part of Turkish territory by Foreign Powers ; and for that reason, an English colony would be admitted with good-will, with trust and confidence to the advantages of Turkish subjects, and be privileged in enjoying the privileges which the rights of a Turkish subject confer.

P.S. The preceeding pages were in the press, when the *Standard* of December 21st inst., brought us the following correspondence from Constantinople, December 14th, than what could be more conclusive in support of our plans and of our warning to the English bondholders of Turkey ?

No further progress has been made since I last wrote towards the accumulation of funds for the payment of the January dividends, and people begin to hint that no more money can be got in from the country, or that the little which may arrive is imperatively required for the war and for other purposes. It is a fact that all the *vilayets* are heavily in arrear, and that the arrears cannot be got in. It is the normal condition of the tax-gatherers to be in arrear, and if they are heavily pressed they have no choice but to admit their insolvency. In the *vilayet* of the Danube last year the tithes only yielded 53 per cent. of their estimated amount. The greater part of the remaining 47 per cent. was left in the hands of the tax-gatherer. At present the *vilayet* of Angora, one of the richest in the Empire, is heavily in arrear. It was expected to remit 240.000 Turkish pounds before the end of this month, but as yet it has only remitted 22,000 (twenty-two thousand out of two hundred and forty thousand) Turkish pounds on account. The mutessanifs and the caimacans of the province have been urged to exert themselves for the recovery of the remainder, but no one expects to succeed. It is my firm belief that Turkey can pay the bondholders nothing for four or five years, and that if they wish to see their money at any future time they had better give her the easiest possible terms, and allow her at least that amount of time for the liquidation of the heavy amount of internal debt which cripples every interest in the country, and for the development of her vast natural resources. She cannot create her agriculture, or work her mines, or call back to life the industries for which she was once famous, without a liberal application of money, and, of course, that money will not bring an immediate return, So long as she is forced to impose an excessive taxation on her subjects, and to withhold the money which is due to all her private creditors, it will be impossible for her to make any satisfactory and permanent provision for the liquidation of her public debt. Her internal difficulties will increase from day to day ; province after province will fall away from her, and the bondholders, after being tantalised from quarter to quarter with trifling instalments of their money, will see the remainder disappear from them altogether."

The *Daily Telegraph* brings in its number of the 22nd of

Dec., a letter dated Constantinople, Dec. 14th, containing the following :—

"I have ridden out to-day for some fifteen miles into the interior, and through a district which, if it had been in the neighbourhood of any other European capital, would have been tended like a garden. As my eye ranged over long lines of hills and valleys, innocent of the plough, and cropped only by a few lean kine and ragged ill-nurtured sheep, I thought of the trim market-gardens by which London and Paris are surrounded, and of the wealth which English and French labour knows how to extract from a soil less fertile and under a sun less propitious than those with which Providence has blessed the Turk. It is customary for sciolists who know nothing of their subjects to say that agriculture in Turkey does not prosper because it has no roads and no markets ; but here, at the doors of Constantinople, we have roads of fair quality, and a market which craves supplies, and which will continue to lack traffic and to languish in the absence of produce, so long as agriculture lies bound hand and foot in the fetters which ignorance, bigotry and chicanery have forged for her. There is not on the face of the earth a more lovely country than this."

In further support of our project we leave the above impartial statements to our readers without comment.

That our opinion concerning the presumptuous intervention of the Powers in the affairs of Turkey is not an isolated one, results from a leading article in the *Daily Telegraph* of Dec. 28th, purporting that,

" The constant intervention of the Consuls or Ambassadors, sometimes for the purpose of removing a really honest Governor, is an element of annoyance to the Porte, and a source of insuperable difficulty in the work of government, but is for that reason greatly cherished by certain of the Powers. The extra-official consular and ambassadorial interference—not the mere legal action of the consular courts—constitute an *imperium in imperio* which, as useful to ambitious purposes and as loosening the homogeneity of the Ottoman Empire, will not be readily given up, whatever professions of solicitude for the welfare of the rayahs it may be found convenient to make for the benefit of a badly informed European opinion.

and, concluding, the *Daily Telegraph* adds :

" We trust the Porte will have the firmness, with the countenance of England, to reject every plan of quasi-tutelage and partial or joint protectorate, and declare that she will rather lose altogether in fair fight a small and unimportant district than consent to hold it on terms which would imperil her sovereign rights over every province in her dominions."

# Turkey's Fall the Decline of England.

~~~~~~~~~~~~~~~~~~~~~~~~~~

THE *Daily Telegraph*, commenting upon the memorandum issued by the Turkish Government on the 20th of October last, suggests that the investors in Turkish Loans are contributing several millions sterling a-year towards the regeneration of the Rayas, and adds, "FROM THIS NOVEL POINT OF VIEW, IN FACT, THE REGENERATOR OF TURKEY IS THE FOREIGN BONDHOLDER."

These words of the *Daily Telegraph* may have been meant to be half or wholly ironical; yet, taken seriously, they contain a great truth,—in fact, the key to the whole situation. They indicate the basis on which the Foreign Bondholders must act, in order, not only to recover their due, but also to contribute mightily, in the evident interest of England, towards the political restoration of the Turkish Empire.

If the millions lent by England to Turkey were lost to-morrow for ever, and yet the legitimate influence and necessary power of the Turkish Empire restored, the loss would be a small one to the English nation, compared to the lasting benefit which would accrue to England from that restoration.

We hope to prove this in the following pages, after having ventured to give the present bondholders some serious advice as to the means of consolidating and making good their claim, and at the same time attaining the goal of what England must always consider as the surest guarantee of her safety in the East.

It is an axiom in the now generally acknowledged principles concerning the liabilities of nations,—a doctrine, in fact, which constitutes a regular system with its determined laws and necessary issues, that *no country can pay its debts otherwise than from its own resources ; and that, if these resources do not keep pace with its liabilities, such a*

*country is on a sure and direct way towards bank-*
*ruptcy.*

It is for the present useless to comment on the recklessness with which bankers, brokers, and the public in general, induced by the prospect or fallacious promises of large profits, have embarked their money in Turkish Loans.

If they had been wise, or simply prudent, they would have satisfied themselves, before parting with their money, as to the real basis on which the demands for credit on the part of the Turkish Government were founded; and would have required to know where and to whom their savings were going, securing at the same time a guarantee for the profitable and reproductive employment of them.

We know very well that to ask such a guarantee would have sounded like an undue interference with the affairs of a country seemingly befriended by England, and would have offended its dignity. But, considered from the side of practical business and sound sense, is it just, we ask, is it right that a Government should be authorised to put their hands into people's pockets under fallacious representations, and promises which they know themselves unable fully to fulfil?

We have already witnessed so many changes for the better in the official management of human affairs during a quarter of a century, that we may in a few years expect greater changes still in that direction; and that the time will soon come when we shall possess Foreign Offices whose chief business and care will be to control all matters concerning and affecting the international interests of the community, and enact such guarantees for international loans as will make the money advanced to foreign Governments almost as secure as if it were in the lenders' pockets.

But that time has not yet come, and meanwhile the best thing we can do is to advise the deluded English shareholders TO HELP THEMSELVES. They have happily to deal with a well-disposed Government and an honest people. The Turks can be certainly upbraided with having imprudently spent the money they so easily obtained; they are far behind us in all that belongs to science, industry, and a well-regulated Government; but they are strictly honest, and whatever may have been alleged against them by the abettors of Rome since the Crusades, and nowadays by Ultramontane zealots, they are essentially tolerant.

They do not try to make proselytes, and they are particularly hostile to proselytism ; if you put aside certain forms, they are *Christians* in the broader and humane acceptance of the word ; but they hate the idolatry of Rome.

If any person looks closely and without prejudice at the barrier between Islamism and Christianity (in the pure and Protestant sense of the word), the separation between both appears simply a thin wooden partition, which has been wickedly represented as a barrier of impassable rocks by Romanism, because of the superiority of the Islam over their own gross idolatry.

There is almost no barrier at present left between us, for polygamy is disappearing fast from among them, and all Turks who lived at the school of Western civilization, were so wrapt up in admiration of our female society, that I myself often heard them curse the motives and prejudices which prevented them from contracting marriages, especially in England.

We have read of late in the papers the fatal result of the fascination exercised by an English lady on a promising Hindoo student of our industry. This is not an isolated case, and we are convinced that frequent intermarriages will bring in a few years the Eastern world near us, on the ground of Protestantism; for all the eminent Turks in Constantinople and elsewhere give their children a splendid education, making their daughters thoroughly unfit for the secluded humiliation of the harem, which will soon be thrown open by the emancipation of women, and by the thorough establishment of monogamy as a necessary consequence of that emancipation.

Let us not forget that *polygamy* was TOLERATED by Mahomet, but not imposed by any law of the Prophet, who was compelled to yield to an inveterate custom of the East, almost as old as the oldest records in the Bible.

We were obliged to enter into these seeming trifles, because they become very serious symptoms if observed nearer, and, in fact, will greatly contribute to prepare the ground for the edifice of which I shall now endeavour to sketch the main outlines.

As Turkey can only by her own means disburden herself from her immensely accumulated debt, it is clear at once to all who know Turkey, that those means are at present inadequate to her wants, and that the only way left open to the shareholders is, to help Turkey to find new means for her present wants, and develop her old ones.

It is beyond doubt that the Turkish Government and the Sultan will be compelled to introduce the strictest economy at Court, and in all branches of administration ; yet, even then, they will not find in the already over-taxed peasantry the considerable resources needed for her present financial difficulties.

And as the Turkish Government must, on that account, feel disposed to meet the shareholders more than half-way in acceding to all proposals by which Turkey would see her burden alleviated, both would easily come to an understanding, based on large concessions on the part of the Sultan.

These concessions could be no other than territorial. Turkey is the land *par excellence* for colonisation, by the richness of her soil and her vast mineral resources, hitherto almost unexplored, or at least not utilised.

Therefore, let the shareholders—the English, we mean—come together, and name a committee of influential men, whose authority would secure the moral co-operation of Government.

That committee would send one or two delegates to Constantinople, in order to examine what concessions on the side of the Porte would be most profitable to the shareholders and most beneficial to Turkey itself.

The committee, after having sounded the Government of the Padishah on its intentions, would further examine what part of Turkey in Europe, to begin with, is most in need of means of transport and communication, and likely to profit most by them, making those means productive at the same time.

For *that* part of Turkey, the committee would come in for a grant of concession of a territory, vast enough to establish a colony of European engineers, mechanics, artisans, and labourers, who would establish tramways for all—wheat-corn and horses abounding in Turkey—with a gauge as broad as that of the Turkish railways, in order to be easily converted into the latter if necessary.

The colonists immigrating from Europe would establish provisory settlements, destined to become railway stations, and, later, villages or small towns ; their inhabitants, Christians or Turks, providing, by their custom to the tramways, a bonus, which would be collected by the company of bond-holders, with a royalty to the Sultan.

Each immigrant workman would receive a piece of ground large enough to live on with his family, and to earn a handsome yearly surplus; and as the association of shareholders would endeavour to secure much more territory than would be necessary in the onset, the thriving workmen could become large farmers, by acquiring with their earned surplus larger portions of ground than that primitively allotted to them.

The jurisdiction of the colonies would be reserved to the colonists themselves at first, by the election of judges, provisorily named from the elder and most respected men of the community.

The colonists would receive from the Association tents, or small wooden houses, so planned as to be easily enlarged when needed; also aratory instruments, and seeds for a year. The question of cattle, to be let out to the colonists, would be settled afterwards.

No taxes of any kind would be levied *during* the first year; but, at the end of it, the colonists would be bound to pay a small sum towards refunding to the Association the advances for the first instalment; as also in the second year another small sum for the same purpose; and so on, till complete extinction of the debt: besides a small ground-rent on the granted property, and the same for twenty consecutive years, when the colonist would become an absolute and independent freeholder of the tenement, liable only to moderate taxes, of which the amount would be settled beforehand between the Company and the Turkish Government.

The colonist working on the tramways would receive his pay half in money and half in cheques, which would be received by the Company in payment of advances made—taxes and ground-rent; as also, later, for the further acquisition of land by the colonists.

The Turkish Government would not only partake of a reasonable share—to be fixed beforehand —in the income of the Company from the conceded lands, the tramways, the mines, quarries, forests, etc., but every shareholder, in exchange of the conceded territory, would consent to liberate the Government of one-half per cent. on the shares of the adjourned debt; which means the one to be repaid provisionally in paper, thus rendering easy for the Sublime Porte the liquidation of her debt.

Shareholders would be admitted by preference to become members of the Association, and entitled to its benefits, accruing from mines, quarries, forests, means of communication, etc.; on which, however, a royalty would be stipulated for the Sultan and his Government.

The colony would be placed under the influence and control of our diplomatic agents in Constantinople, who, together with the representatives of the German Empire, are highly respected there; the latter being moreover interested as much as England in the prosperity and *integrity* of Turkey as a political power.

We mean also to say, that if Germany were to

send colonists to the English establishment, the fact would meet with high approval from the German official world.

It would not be desirable to recruit or admit colonists of the Roman creed, their rites being in the highest degree offensive to Mussulmans, who, at the same time, detest riots and drunkenness,—both concomitants, as we all know, of Irish emigrants, wherever they go.

The colonists of Roman creed ought to be settled apart, in villages remote from any Mussulman community; the more as their priests are dangerous meddlers and busybodies, succeeding absolutely in nothing but in creating difficulties for the countries of which they are subjects,—as the French have experienced in Algeria, in China, and elsewhere.

We want to live in peace with the Moslems, and befriend them; and the English rule in India has shown long years since how such things can be managed.

Protestant Holland has lived in peace and done good business with Japan under a thousand more obstacles than we ever shall meet with amongst the relatively civilized Turkish peasantry, who are peaceful, kind, intelligent, and open to all that could alleviate their hard condition.

And *that* we can and will do, by the best of proselytism and propaganda : good examples in behaviour, in husbandry, in all those superior arts of which an Englishman is justly proud, and by which he is sure to command the confidence and even moral allegiance of the hitherto diffident and prejudiced Moslem.

We are not come to preach new doctrines ; the doctrines of England and her statesmen are liberal, especially in all that relates to foreign nations, and they keep pace with the progress of the age. Yet we have of late witnessed a salutary authoritative interference in foreign politics on the side of England, which will exercise the highest influence over the whole political and financial world.

Alderman Cotton, the new Lord Mayor elect, has inaugurated a policy which we would call extra-official, if the Lord Mayor of London was not representing the mighty London city with the same authority as the Government issued from

Parliament represents the English nation. He has banished from the time-honoured festivities of the Guildhall the representatives of those States which have acted dishonestly towards the English nation, but he has not excluded Turkey; and that was right, for Turkey has only postponed the payment of her debt, for which her resources offer a certain guarantee, if properly managed, as by good and timely advice they have every chance to be.

The interference on the part of the highest city magistrate, by shutting the gates of the Guildhall against defaulters, on whom the doors of all the magnates of the city are closed, is a warning which will turn to the lasting honour of the Lord Mayor elect, and give the borrowing States a hint which will be lost neither on the borrowers nor on the lenders.

Let us now animadvert to the probable, almost certain, result of a vast European colony in Turkey.

The example of skill and thrift put by English hands to the Turkish peasantry will produce the best consequences. The Turkish peasant, relieved of ruining taxes, will strive to become happy, wealthy, comfortable, like the men come from the west to teach him how to appreciate and bless better laws, a better administering of them, a juster and more equitable re-partition of benefits between the master and the subject.

Nor is this all; for the future destinies of Turkey will interest thousands of Englishmen; some from the mere interest of their money, but others, and a greater number, from higher patriotic feelings and from foresight in national politics.

That Russia is slowly advancing towards Constantinople, as well as towards the English Empire in the East, is as evident as is the light of the sun. If ever Russia ruled at Constantinople, England would descend to the rank of a third-rate power; for, the possession of Constantinople is the key of the Empire over India and Egypt. From Constantinople, the Czar, arrived at the summit of Russian ambition, may cry out in his triumph, *Super et Garamantas et Indos preferem imperium!*

Napoleon I. used to say that Constantinople was the key of European domination. Times have changed, it is true: America has become that which Napoleon could neither have foreseen nor, if foreseen, understood; but what he said then is true to this very day. If Russia reigns on the Bosphorus, English rule is fatally doomed.

England may be proud of her immense influence in the world,—not due, like once the Spanish supremacy, to coined gold, exacted from the new world, but to her industry, which made the world a willing tributary of a supremacy which can never be humbled as long as England is prominent by her energy for commerce, industry, liberty at home and abroad, and for her conscience of rights which she must never abandon, of duties which she must always manfully fulfil, come of it what may.

It is therefore our duty to consider what is the real state of Russia, in order to know what we have to hope and what to fear.

We have, in the way of better views and sounder appreciation of our interests, gained *this* advantage—that we would no longer consent to destroy the Turkish fleet, as we did like dupes of Russia, and of the ill-timed sentimentality of Lord Byron and other so-called Philhellenists, in a second battle of Navarino.

England has made war against Russia with

France for ally, and a few days ago one of the most heroic deeds of history has been recalled to the memory of Englishmen, by the celebration of the heroic fight at Balaklava.

And what was the conduct of Russia and of her whilom adversary, Napoleon III. allied with England, after the conclusion of the Crimean war?

The first care of Russia was to gain back by her diplomacy what she had lost in the field; and her success was complete, for Napoleon III., the *parvenu*, proud of having humiliated Russia, whose Emperor, refusing to call him *brother*, qualified him simply but reluctantly *his friend*, was easily duped *enguirlandé*, as the Russians call it; and his enemy became more powerful than ever by the Treaty of Paris, in which the allies gave up everything to the arbitrary caprice of Russia without any earthly guarantee for themselves, as the later results have proved.

Before that issue people had thought that with the death of Nicholas the feud would die out, and that Alexander, his successor, would be tractable and pacific; but it proved precisely the contrary.

Alexander called the whole nation to arms, sharing in every respect the opinions of his brother Constantine ; and it was only when the protracted ruinous war, the prostration of Russian trade, and the dearth of all commodities, had brought to resipiscence the Russian nobility and the commercial community; when all Russia lingered for peace, that the Czar at last gave in, when the conquest of Kars seemed to atone for the fall of Sebastopol, and a secret understanding with Napoleon III. had made him sure of getting the most advantageous conditions of peace.

What is going to follow is mainly borrowed from, or inspired by, German historians, travellers, philosophers, as to what concerns Russia ; and they are well known and deservedly esteemed in England for their conscientious researches, their accuracy, and their veracity in statements.

After the Treaty of Paris, Russia evidently favours the projects of France on Italy ; not in the interest of Napoleon III., but with the aim of humiliating her hereditary enemy, Austria.

Russia thought that a simulated cordial understanding with France would overawe Europe.

England could but with jealousy view it, and Prussia was docile to Russian dictates.

Immediately after the conclusion of peace, Alexander went to Varsovia to grant the Poles a constitution, and warn them, at the same time, against what he called *dangerous illusions.*

From Varsovia the Czar went to Berlin, on the 26th of May, 1865, to strengthen the old and intimate alliance between the Romanows and the Hohenzollern.

And, in fact, the Czar could not thank enough the King of Prussia for his neutrality during the war, and for having dissuaded Austria from joining the allies, keeping at the same time aloof from the treaty of the 15th April of the same year.

And yet that conduct had not been approved but even blamed by Germany, whose people hate Russia most cordially.

The Emperor did not go beyond Berlin, but his mother, Nicholas's widow, went soon afterwards to visit her daughter, Princess Olga, who became, later, the queen of Würtemberg. The Empress squandered immense sums on the penurious peasants of Würtemberg, trying to prove that the

Russian finances had not suffered by the war,—a rather transparent fiction, as it was notorious that the money spent by the Empress Dowager had cost fifteen and even twenty per cent.

But that did not satisfy completely enough Russian pride and hypocrisy. Alexander had resolved to be crowned at Moscow. The solemnity took place on the 7th of September, 1856, in the presence of all the foreign ambassadors.

Alexander had assembled for this ceremony 200,000 men, the flower of the Russian army; and the envoys of foreign powers were compelled to witness the act of defiance thrown in the face of astonished Europe.

A great number of German princes and princesses had come there, to be eclipsed by the pomp of foreign ambassadors.

But the humiliation of the latter was to be absolute, complete.

In midst of the foreigners and of the high dignitaries of the Russian Court appeared suddenly the representatives of the various provinces which form the immense Russian Empire—imposing figures, who seemed to belong to another age, an heroic world long forgotten; men with a proud look and a disdainful mien, but resplendent with jewels.

The eye met groups like this—one hundred horsemen mounting magnificent steeds, and wearing the richest and most varied costumes; they were headed by an old man completely covered with gold embroideries. It was Prince Schtscherbatoff, marshal of the nobility of the Government of Moscow.

They were the Boyards of the Empire, in their national costumes, wearing the *insignia* of their respective dignities. They were the descendants of the mighty men who in olden times governed the Empire conjointly with the Czars, and who were mentioned often in the Ukases as having agreed to what the Czar had decreed under the approbation of the Patriarch.

Since Peter, nicknamed the Great, the power of these Boyards has been curtailed; but it is still considerable, for every one commands over thousands and some over hundreds of thousands of serfs.

The partial emancipation of the serfs has struck a deadly blow to their influence, and it is almost certain that the measures taken by the Czars since three reigns towards that emancipation, were not ordered out of humanity, nor from the desire or foresight of founding a powerful state on the happiness and prosperity of a free people, but with the aim of crushing the power of the ancient nobility of the Empire, so averse in their national pride to a foreign dynasty.

But all the vanities and pomp accumulated on the 7th of September, 1856—all the embroideries, all the jewels displayed, covered hideous ulcers, affecting the whole body politic of the Empire like a leprosy.

For the Czar bears, in the eyes of the Russian people—so jealous and proud of their nationality —a stigma which nothing can ever efface. All the members of the present reigning dynasty are descendants of Peter III., who came from Holstein, and was, consequently, a German; and of his wife, Catherine II., who came from Anhalt, and was a German; so that the Roumanows of to-day have not a single drop of Russian blood in their veins.

All the dignitaries who surrounded the Czar on

that memorable day were, and *are still*, night and day open to conspiracies like those which have so often shaken, and sometimes nearly overthrown, the dynasty of the foreign Czars, who, in the eyes of the Muscovites, are nothing better than usurpers.

All the powerful magnates of Muscovy hate the Czars; and their presence in St. Petersburg, the new capital of the Empire, is particularly galling to them, as they pretend that Moscow should be the Imperial residence, as it always had been before Peter I. transferred the seat of the Government to St. Petersburg.

Ardent, enthusiastic writers oppose the Government on a ground which we shall call Moscovitism, and which must cause Alexander many a sleepless night. There is but one element of unity in Russia—"the Ranks"; and to keep these ranks in order, the Government has but two means at its disposal—the KNOUT, and Siberia.

The Government has, since Alexander II. came to the throne, committed faults which may be considered as the outset of a general cataclysm in Russia.

The emancipation of the serfs was resorted to with a dangerous precipitation, and it resulted in a perilous application of a maxim of Russian rule.

In times when serfs were an integral part of the soil, *adscripti glebæ*, the rural commune or parish possessed in common a certain portion of land, considered as communal and collective property, because the lord of the soil, the nobleman, was bound to find his peasants.

From time to time, the parish distributed her land in such way that the father of a family received a portion, of more or less extent, according to the men of which he could dispose for the culture of it; and, conforming to a law founded on long custom, it was determined what quantity of ground was to be allotted to each individual.

This custom favours extremely the doctrines of socialism and communism, as it corresponds to the principle after which the parish, being at the same time the landlord, has no right to let the individual who lives upon it starve. Another consequence of that system was, that the Government taxed the communes collectively, and not its inhabitants individually; which induced the parish to deliver over to the Czar, for his army, her profligate and destitute members, and keep the good working men; for the more active men there were in the parish the easier became the collecting of taxes.

At the emancipation of the serfs, the property which had been allotted to the parishes was taken away from them; the Government maintaining, nevertheless, the duty for them to pay collectively the taxes. This was at once decreeing black and white.

The Government declares arbitrarily that such and such a parish numbering so many individuals, the whole of them will pay solidarily a fixed amount of taxes, thus enacting the rule that it is not the individual but the whole commune which is liable for them.

Let us admit—and in fact it is the common rule —that half of the parish is composed of good-for-nothing individuals; the consequence must be that orderly hard-working men pay for them. And, supposing a possible and probable case, that the whole parish be composed of a set of loafers, it would necessarily ensue, if only two hard-working men were to live in it, these two would be compelled to pay for all the rest. No doubt the commune can come down on the good-for-nothings and make them pay, but she is deprived of her former means of coercion.

The lazy profligate can do nothing with the land, as he does not cultivate it; and he laughs when they take away from him by law that which is of no value to him.

It is difficult to find in Russia people who will consent to become agricultural labourers. Agriculture is abhorred in Russia, and that is another reason why the industrious man must work for the profligate; for what could a man do with the land he has taken from the profligate for debt, if he can neither cultivate it himself nor have it tilled by others for want of willing hands?

And it is thus that the industrious man loses all courage, becoming soon lazy and indifferent himself.

Since Russia entered the paths of judicial reforms, she possesses, it is true, Justices of Peace, whom their high salary makes independent. But the Government places at the side of an act of wisdom, an act of downright folly, by decreeing that the Justices of Peace be submitted every three years to a popular re-election, and then of course, such as have proved too severe in the opinion of the majority—which is composed, as we have seen, of loafers and idlers—lose their lucrative position, to be replaced by magistrates esteemed more supple, more corrupt, more disposed to make law a mockery.

It will happen, for example, that an individual shall drive his pigs in a field of corn belonging to his neighbour, not out of any malice, but because it was more handy for him ; or a servant engaged by contract to a master, will keep away from him and amuse himself for three or four days. The Justice of Peace, proclaiming the *minimis non curat Pretor*, overlooks such trifles for fear of losing his popularity, which means his daily bread.

Is it, then, a wonder that the number of gin houses has grown to such an extent that there are districts where we count as many as one for every group of 100 or 125 inhabitants, and that the dealers in gin clear from their houses annual profits usually amounting to 2000 roubles?

Who could hear of such a state of things without the utmost disgust and indignation?

No man of honour, no civilized man, except such as the raving Russian publicist Katkow, who calls THAT order of things the *non plus ultra* of a well-conducted state, and has such monstrosities printed in his *Gazette de Moscow*, and the Government believes them, or feigns to believe them, and feels disposed to glorify in his own wickedness and folly.

But the consequences of such a blindness become soon conspicuous.

The serf, ruined by his own laziness and by drink, seeing how some of his comrades had got on better, was reminded of the periodical allotment of land. His former landlord was no longer bound to keep him, it is true, but the crown had bought him, and he considered himself logically as the property of the Emperor, and according to that primitive simple conclusion he believes in his right to claim that the Emperor keep him as his former landlord did. And that very man thinks that the Emperor ought to order now and then a re-allotment of land. In short, he deems that the Czar must take from the rich the means of keeping drunkards and idlers.

And it is in a soil thus prepared that the Russian socialist, the revolutionary Bakounine, sows the seed of a doctrine which, as it is developed and spread, becomes the terror of the Russian Government and of the foreign dynasty which rules supreme and absolute in Russia.

Wherever you look out on Russia, its future is a mysterious and dark one to the eye of the statesman deserving that name, and nobody can foresee what evil the order of. things obtaining in that enigmatic country may bring on herself and the other States of the Continent.

The Russian expeditions in Asia, having no other aim than to flatter Muscovite ambition and to blindfold the people, under the pretence of conquests, must, in the long run, prove sterile; because Russia has no genius for colonisation, no genius for order, progress, or sound administration. The Russians have *aptitudes* and ambition, but no higher vocation, no higher aspiration than brutal savage conquest. Love of mankind, of the welfare of nations, is a stranger to them, and their ideas of liberty do not extend beyond low vulgar license. As to Russian industry, it is so backward that the Russians themselves, when they speak of indifferent products of industry, call them scornfully RUSSIAN WORKMANSHIP.

And yet, to such a Government, based on nothing but pomp, vanity, hypocrisy and corruption, we open wide the doors of our strong-boxes; we give our money to build railways, that she might the easier throw her savage hordes, headed by German adventurers, on Turkey and from Turkey, on the English possessions in India.

The actual order of things in Russia—government and dynasty—must and will be overthrown by a terrible revolution, fomented by the Muscovite party and aided by peasants imbued with the deleterious doctrines of Communism.

If Moscovitism triumphs, as it must finally, it will surely repudiate the debts made by a Government which the Muscovite magnates declare anti-national, foreign, and without any root in the nation.

There is perhaps not a loan—not even a Honduras one—that inspires us with less confidence than the Russian loans,—completely, absolutely void as they are of every possible or even probable guarantee.

What resource would the English bondholders have if Russia repudiated her debt?—which, in reality, she is no more able to pay than overburdened Turkey. None, for the English Government would not wage war on behalf of the robbed and ruined bondholders, although it would have gone to war with China for the murder of an inferior diplomatic agent.

We predict to the English bondholders the bankruptcy of the present order of things in Russia, because Russia must come, inevitably, to a terrible revolution.

Exercise too high a pressure on a steam boiler, and it will burst. Indulge in too high a compression of the legitimate wish and demands, or even the honourable prejudices, of a nation, and that nation will fatally explode by a revolution, shattering to atoms the despotism and usurpation which thought themselves secure behind what they deemed an impregnable fortress—coercion and enslavement in all its forms.

Russia has already seen many so-called palace revolutions; let its dynasty beware of "the Forest of Dunsinane," marching fatally on St. Petersburg to storm and destroy the castle of Macbeth.

After the oppression of dull Metternich's political, or rather police system, Austria came to a revolution, and overthrew her antique dynasty. The duller Charles X. brought over France the unnecessary curse of a new revolution by the silly ordinances of July, 1830.

And why was England safe from similar catastrophes, when the Continent was trembling on its basis? And why will it remain free from revolutions, perhaps for ever? Because of the superiority of her statesmen and the wisdom of her twofold senate. Because the higher classes, instead of stubbornly sticking to principles which time has matured into prejudices, give way to the general ideas and aspirations of their people and the age; because, instead of acting on the impulse of necessity, they honour and exalt their high station by taking the lead of all measures commanded by the spreading knowledge of the conditions of welfare, both moral and material, for mankind, for their nation, for MAN.

And as the senate acts *in corpóre*, so do the individual members of the nobility. During the last few days we saw a mighty peer apologize for a blunder which he made by giving vent to an untimed prejudice. This apology to public opinion honoured him more than any other act of his career.

English statesmen at the head of foreign affairs act on the same principle as in their interior policy. It will be the eternal honour of Lord Palmerston, and its greatest and proudest title to the gratitude of all nations, that he, a peer, gave up the ancient Tory traditions in foreign affairs, to support the cause of liberty against despotism all over the world.

The nearer a country approaches the liberal institutions, and adopts the liberal views of England as possessing a Government strong by the welfare of the people, backed by the latter, and knowing no other pride, indulging in no other boast than its prosperity,—to those countries we can entrust our money: France, Belgium,

Holland, Germany, the United States, and, to a certain extent, Italy.

THAT must be the barometer of all financial men, who, as honest men and Englishmen, consider their wealth, not as a hoard they can dispose of arbitrarily, or like the Prodigal Son of Scripture, but as a part of the wealth and weal of the nation, and as such to be managed and spent with foresight and caution.

If a profligate, a spendthrift, after having got through with his estates, knocked at the door of an industrious banker or merchant for a loan, the man of business would politely hold to him the language of the thrifty ant of the fable to the light-headed grasshopper.

And yet, when profligate, spendthrift, or deeply devising Governments come to the powerful *financiers* of the city with an empty purse, and emptier titles and promises, the *financiers* throw their doors wide open, invite them inside, and beg them to consider their strong-box as belonging, not to the owner, but to the borrowing spendthrift; and that is the fact, for a Potentate reigning and governing on a volcano, offers no guarantee of solvability; and we

should like to know if the Muscovite party over-
throwing the present Romanow dynasty, with the
deluded and degraded peasantry at their back, would
hesitate a moment to repudiate debts made by the
German dynasty, with no other guarantee or value
than the paper on which the bonds of debt are
printed.

When the blood runs to the head, is it not the fore-
boding of apoplexy ? It does nothing else, and will
never do anything else in Russia mayhap for centuries.

But it depends on us to make the blood run healthily
in the body of the Turkish Empire, by bringing it
down from the head to all its veins and arteries.

An English contemporary has given the advice to
annex Egypt, as a security of eventual changes at
Constantinople,—for example, a protectorate of
Russia ; and recent events in Asia have shown us too
clearly what Russian protectorate means, not in the
long, but in the very short run.

England could not possibly be induced into a more
impolitic, nay, more criminal blunder, by which it
would plunge herself blindly, headlong, inevitably into
a general war.

Let us once for all consider on what general principle of wise and expedient policy Egypt must be maintained as an independent state.

All the nations of the globe have a common interest in that great and beneficial enterprise, the canal of Suez; and no nation can consent to let that work of universal utility, with which no one would henceforth dispense, become the exclusive property of any single nation, and the probable object and occasion of a dangerous menacing monopoly.

Taking in account the particular reasons for having Egypt free and independent, as an impartial watch over the shortest road to the East, we find, first, that England must not feel disposed to annihilate the most devoted ally she has.

France would never willingly consent to an annexion of Egypt by England, which cannot feel inclined to make the best of the distress of her neighbour to wound him to the heart by such an act of iniquity.

And what if such act provoked on the part of France, who hitherto stuck faithfully to the English alliance, a resentment which would bring on a political understanding between her and Russia?

Those who think that France is maimed are wholly

unacquainted with the real state of things. Prince Bismarck may have thought so, and acted upon it; but his overbearing may once cost him dear.

Neither the United States, nor Germany, nor Italy, nor the Minor States,—like Sweden, Denmark, Holland, and even Spain and Portugal,—would give their *fiat* to the possession of Egypt by England, who already exercises there all the power it can wish to pretend to; highly beneficial, we confess, to the welfare of Egypt.

Englishmen explore for her, unknown regions; extend her sway over barbarous countries; command and discipline her army; build and man her ships; establish their railways and manufactures.

They are consulted in all things, and listened to with deference by the Viceroy. What can England wish beyond it, and what could she do more even if she exercised a complete, established patronage over that State?

War and violence have never borne fruits either to nations or to individuals. Let us endeavour to become in Turkey what we have become in Egypt, under infinitely greater obstacles; and let it be not only at the head, but also at the basis of the State.

The only means of doing it is—to propagate at Constantinople advices like those which have brought thither Mr. Scudamore, and which would have brought there our great statesman, the Right Hon. W. E. Gladstone, if he had not felt what insuperable difficulties he would have to contend with on a ground which was not prepared for the first steps he would feel obliged to take, and which would have probably, in such conditions, met with a failure. But that is, for the present at least, of less consequence. The Sultan, who seems to be a rather money-hunting or cunning gentleman, may have been induced to invite Mr. Scudamore from hearing what vast resources the English exchequer derived from the post and the telegraphs, and have had simply in view an accruing of resources for his Treasury. But what of that also for the present? Could the Sultan be induced to invite to Constantinople a dozen practical English administrators for the same motives, Turkish sovereigns, whoever they might be, would learn that it is their direct interest to enrich and not to rob and impoverish their subjects, whose labour and thrift alone can fill their exchequer and make the sovereign really powerful and respected.

By doing the contrary of Russia, by encouraging instead of discouraging the peasantry, the Sultans would oppose the strongest and safest barrier against Russian encroachments.

But another political project than that of annexing Egypt has been ventilated in the English press, viz., the favouring the independent aspirations of Roumania, Servia, Montenegro, and the Herzegovina.

Whoever knows these countries well, knows at the same time that it would be equivalent to throwing them as a ready prey to Russia, whose Government, by lavishing money on the prominent beggars of those Principalities, exercises already, in concurrence with Austria, who strives on towards the same goal, a real protectorate over those small but important communities. Guarantees ought certainly to be given by the Porte for a more equitable government over her non-Moslem subjects in those countries, but nothing more. The lowest Turk is far superior to these debased wretches, whose inferiority and wicked cunning inspires the Moslem with that contempt of which they complain, and which Austrians or Russians, if they ever ruled over them, would feel tenfold stronger.

Years will pass before any light will penetrate into that abyss of darkness and abjection.

A *modus vivendi* could easily be found between the Turks and them, provided that *modus vivendi* were drawn up by England, and not by hypocritical and deceitful Russia, or by sneaky and, in these questions still, Jesuitical Austria.

We have seen above what could be done in Turkey at the summit of the State. Let us now go back again to the basis.

Here, the only remedy are colonies. We hear from certain sources that the Mormons, tracked by the Government of the United States, have, as it was advised to them to do long ago, resolved to seek refuge in Turkey, where they will be received, as we are assured, with open arms. The wonders they did in converting sterile tracts into fertile land, will certainly plead their cause in Turkey, where the former Sultan had conceded a large territory to the French poet Lamartine, out of which he could never make anything for want of capital and able colonists, which French people are certainly not.

And would it not be a shame for England to see a non-Christian sect like the Mormons take root and thrive in Turkey, and they, Englishmen, who devote hundreds of thousands a year for the propagation of the Bible, and of Christian faith, look on to such a probable result with absolute indifference, when they could be realizing the simple plan indicated, and which is realizable by mere small profitable advances and without any possible loss?

Such a conclusion seems to us impossible, and contrary to the genius and to the high religious feelings of the English people.

The Sultan would be most happy to concede suitable tracts of land for the colonisation of Turkish territory, the more as it would tend to conciliate the most influential of his bondholders.

But let us not pass lightly over the conditions on which alone such establishments can succeed and thrive.

Let our first colonists be engineers, mechanics, agricultural labourers, and good religious men; but let these latter not engage in a proselytism which our long experience has taught us to be utterly sterile all over the Mahometan world. Let us act on the principle of that Scotch colony which went out to the lands disclosed to us by Livingstone with engineers, artizans, labourers, and religious men.

If our missionaries want to make propaganda, let them work by example ; they are sure to exercise the highest influence over the Turks, whom the overburden of taxes makes indolent, but who are intelligent, skilful, and accessible to all that is noble and generous. Let, therefore, all and every one of our religious men study sedulously medicine and surgery,—two sciences which will open the door wide of every Turkish family deprived in their hardships of every medical aid. Christ was a Divine physician, and it was by His miracles that He got the strongest hold on the unbelievers. It would be blasphemy to think of reviving *His* cures by mortal men ; but, by our Creator's endless bounty, man has been, by his intelligence, capable of revealing and discovering the Divine science for curing, within the bounds of mortality, our earthly evils and misery; and to that science and superiority of the West, Turks and Mussulmans in general are more open to begin with than to any other propaganda.

Let the wives of these missionaries busy themselves Christianly about the welfare of Turkish wives and children, become their teachers and advisers for husbandry, and the like useful arts, which enliven the households of our countries. They will so convert more souls to our truths by the force of example, than all the missionaries could by their well-meant but not readily-understood teaching.

Let us ascend from the plain to the mountain, instead of descending from the hill to the valley. The former method is the safest. Let us not force ourselves on these people; they will come to us by the mere magnetic attraction of good example.

Every Englishman is justly proud of what was done by Englishwomen in the Crimea, with Miss Nightingale at their head. The Turks, to this day, admire and venerate her, whose name in their language is *Bulbul*, as Lady Montague tells us in her charming letters; and if Miss Nightingale appeared suddenly in the midst of the ranks of the Turkish army, or simply in the streets of Constantinople, and she was named and pointed out, she would meet with the same enthusiasm as if she were a sovereign, or with devotion as an envoy to this earth from the land of mercy on a mission of charity and self-sacrifice.

We hope that this appeal will be heard by all noble

philanthropic and high-minded Englishmen and English ladies ; and we are resolved to tell them one great truth, openly, manfully, which a long experience has taught and demonstrated to us. The immense sums expended by England for the propagation of the Scriptures have not attained the aims of the pious and well-meaning donors, because giving a book is not imparting the means of understanding it; and the spreading of the Holy Bible ought to have ended where it begins, viz., the ground of its reception be duly prepared ; the doctrine first preached by example; and then, the book which consecrates it.

The Catholic propaganda has never succeeded but with those poor people, especially negroes, who were pagans, and whose paganism they replaced by another,—the paganism of Rome.

Never did the Roman propaganda dream even of liberating from their inhuman masters the slaves,—whom, it is true, she had herself enslaved in her superstitions. Their missionaries contented themselves with preaching the slaves' resignation to the despotism of inhuman masters, the negro-drivers, the dregs and abomination of mankind. The Protestant missionary preached the Gospel and emancipation.

In China, the Roman missionaries established a system of baptism which was a regular mockery. Wherever they found a child, they baptized it with the simple sign of the cross, conferring on the lowest and most ignorant the power of doing the same,—for a consideration ; and they made mockery of christening new-born children a means of exacting from the Catholic population of Europe—England being a large contributor—enormous sums, which ran, by some channel or other, to the dark and mischievous work of the Jesuits.

To give the Roman Church good advice, is trying to wash a negro, and with the same success.

We do her too much honour in ever noticing the ridiculous pretensions of a body which, like a burnt-out candle-light, throws some vivid flashes before it dies.

The Protestant faith must and will triumph all over the world, but Protestant missionaries must add human science—which, after all, is of Divine origin—to theological attainments. They will thus establish on a lasting basis England's supremacy in Divine doctrine as well as in human wisdom.